Creative Keyboard Presents

Great Women Composers

By Gail Smith

A recording of the music in this book is now available. The publisher strongly recommends the use of this recording along with the text to insure accuracy of interpretation and ease in learning.

Contents ────────────────────────────

Foreword

This book contains a unique sampling of music composed by eleven distinguished woman composers. It spans almost one thousand years in the history of music. Each woman had an interesting life, starting with Hildegard von Bingen and ending with Amy Beach. You will find a variety of musical styles represented by these composers of the past and one new piano solo I've composed.

It was not (and is not) easy for women to have a profession in composing, yet the music of these eleven women has remained classic. Each was held in high esteem during her lifetime.

Nature provides the artist with rainbows, the moon and stars, sunsets, oceans, and everything the eye can behold and reproduce on canvas. The composer can also be inspired by nature and express feelings and deep emotions through the musical score. Try to capture the feelings of these eleven women, then express their music and let it speak to your heart.

One last thought. It is better to be happy over what has been included than to mourn over what has been excluded. I hope you enjoy the twenty-seven selections.

Gail Smith

Hildegard von Bingen ———————

(1098–1179)

Hildegard von Bingen was born in Bemersheim, Germany, in 1098 and died on September 17, 1179, near Bingen, Germany. She is the first woman composer whose music is extant today. Hildegard is considered the greatest woman of the Middle Ages.

Hildegard entered a convent at the age of eight and began her education. Her parents were noble and devout and had promised their tenth child to the church as a tithe. She amazed her teachers at an early age with her visions, prophecies, and miracles. Hildegard was even consulted by emperors, kings, priests, archbishops, and two popes: Anastasius IV and Adrian IV.

When Hildegard was fifteen she became a nun. It was then that she began to write some of the most brilliant poetry of the age. She set seventy-seven poems to music and also wrote a morality play in dramatic verse: "The Order of the Virtues."

Though it was never made official, September 17 is Saint Hildegard's Day in the book of Saints' Days.

Hildegard von Bingen   5

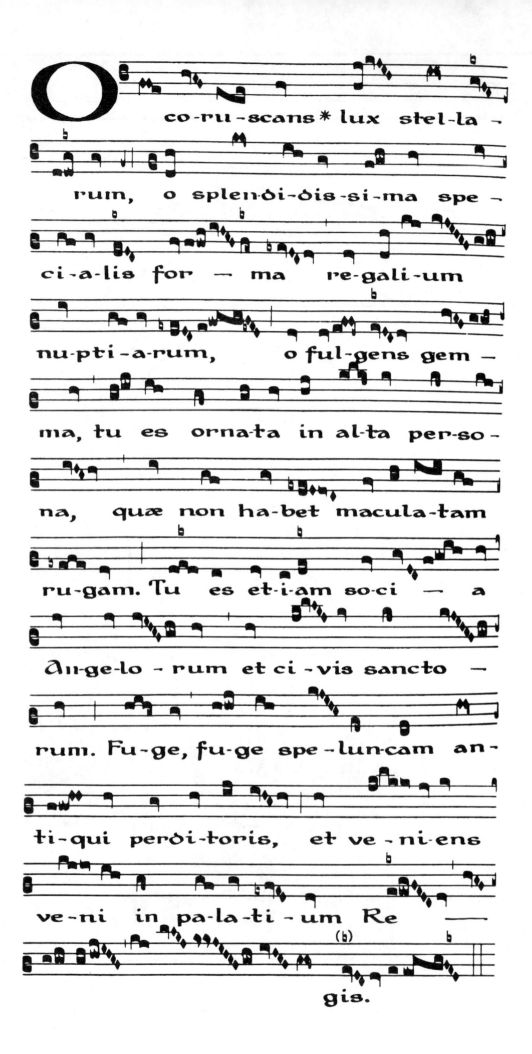

O co-ru-scans* lux stel-la-rum, o splen-di-dis-si-ma spe-ci-a-lis for — ma re-gali-um nu-pti-a-rum, o ful-gens gem — ma, tu es orna-ta in al-ta per-so-na, quæ non ha-bet macula-tam ru-gam. Tu es et-i-am so-ci — a An-ge-lo — rum et ci -vis sancto — rum. Fu-ge, fu-ge spe-lun-cam an-ti-qui per-di-toris, et ve-ni-ens ve-ni in pa-la-ti-um Re — gis.

O Choruscans lux stellarum

Hildegard von Bingen (1098–1179)
Transcribed for piano solo by Gail Smith

Elisabeth-Claude Jacquet de La Guerre ——

(1666–1729)

Elisabeth-Claude Jacquet de La Guerre, a French composer, was born in Paris in 1666. She was born into a family of professional musicians. A precocious child, she started playing the piano at age five and was presented at court to Louis XIV. She dedicated the songs she composed to him. At the age of ten she went to Versailles, where she played a pastoral she had composed. The king liked it so much that he asked to hear it repeated several times. Her manuscripts were kept in his private library, where they remained unpublished. Unfortunately, most of her work was destroyed during the French Revolution.

When Elisabeth was about fifteen years old, Mme. de Montespan took control of her education. Elisabeth had a remarkable talent for improvisation that made her very popular to all. She was married in 1687 to Marin de La Guerre, the organist of St. Louis des jesuites, St. Severin. Soon after her marriage, Elisabeth published her first book, which was a collection of clavecin pieces. She continued to compose many works during her marriage. Her husband died in 1704. In 1707 she published a set of six sonatas for violin and figured bass, along with fourteen movements for harpsichord solo. Elisabeth continued giving concerts until about 1717.

She composed a te deum, for full choir, sung in the Chapel of the Louvre in 1721 to celebrate the recovery from smallpox of Louis XV. Her two books of biblical contatas were among the first to be published in France in the eighteenth century, when this form was in vogue.

Elisabeth died in Paris on June 27, 1729, and was buried in the parish church of St. Eustache. She was one of the first women to compose in such a wide variety of genres and to be recognized for her achievements.

Pictured here are medals that King Louis XIV made in her honor.

Rondeau

Elisabeth-Claude Jacquet De La Guerre (1666–1729)

Notation:

1er Couplet

2e Couplet

Pièces de Clavecin

Elisabeth-Claude Jacquet De La Guerre (1666–1729)

La Flamande

[segue]

Double

2e fois

14   Elisabeth-Claude Jacquet De La Guerre

Chaconne

4.ᵉ Couplet

5.ᵉ Couplet

On reprend le I.ᵉʳ Couplet

Marianne von Martinez

(1744–1812)

Marianne von Martinez was born in Vienna, Austria, on May 4, 1744. Her father, a Neapolitan of Spanish descent, was master of ceremonies to the Pope's Nuncio. Metastasio was a close friend of her father and lived with the family for fifty years. He recognized her talent early on and undertook to have her educated properly. Haydn, then poor and unknown, occupied a garret in the same house and taught her to play the harpsichord. Marianne was in her teens when a mass she composed was performed at the court chapel of St. Michael's. Porpora, a famous Italian composition and singing teacher, gave her lessons.

After her parents and Metastasio died, Marianne and her sister were left a large sum of money. They began giving evening parties and concerts that were frequented by all the principal artists of the day. One evening Mozart came to her party and performed his four-hand sonata with Marianne.

Marianne devoted most of her time to composing and teaching talented pupils. She composed numerous secular and sacred vocal works, a symphony, two keyboard concertos, and two sonatas. Marianne founded a singing school. One of her good friends was the blind composer Maria Theresia von Paradis.

Marianne died on December 13, 1812, a few days after the death of her younger sister, Antonie.

Sonata in E Major

Marianne von Martinez (1744–1812)

Sonata in A Major

Marianne von Martinez (1744–1812)

Tempo di Minuetto

Maria Theresia Von Paradis

(1759–1824)

Maria Theresia Von Paradis was born in Vienna, Austria, on May 15, 1759. Her father was the Viennese Imperal Court Secretary, Josef von Paradis. Maria was named after her godmother, the Empress Maria Theresa. She became blind at the age of two. It was soon discovered that she had great musical talent, and fortunately Maria received an excellent musical education. She developed a great ear for music and learned more than sixty piano concertos by memory. Antonio Salieri was one of her teachers. Maria sang and accompanied herself on the piano. Salieri was so pleased with her abilities that he wrote an organ concerto in her honor.

At first Maria dictated her own compositions but soon devised a special composition board with pegs of various shapes and sizes that she used to put her ideas down.

The famous doctor-hypnotist, Anton Mesmer, treated Maria between 1777 and 1778. For a brief time she regained her sight, but she lost her musical abilities. She was able to compose again only after her blindness returned. (Our word *mesmerized* comes from her doctor, Mesmer.)

In 1783 Marie began a European tour that took her to Paris, London, Hamburg, Berlin, Prague, and Salzburg. Mozart was so impressed with her playing that he wrote a piano concerto for one of her Paris concerts. Unfortunately, the Concerto in B-flat did not reach her in time, and she never performed it. She ended her concert tour in 1786 and returned to Vienna. Maria stopped giving public concerts in the 1790s.

In 1808 Maria founded a music school for handicapped girls whose Sunday concerts drew many of the Viennese society crowd. She spent her remaining years teaching and composing. Her works include three cantatas for full chorus, soloists, and orchestra and over thirty sonatas and combined chamber works for piano and other instruments.

She died on February 11, 1824, in Vienna.

Sicilienne

Maria Theresia Von Paradis (1759–1824)
(for flute and piano, arranged for piano solo by Gail Smith)

Maria Agata Szymanowska

(1789–1831)

aria Agata Szymanowska was a contemporary of Beethoven and Schubert and the first significant Polish pianist and composer of her time. Maria was born in Poland in 1789 and died in 1831. She was a very precocious child and would entertain the family and friends with her improvisations at the keyboard. She was a student of Haydn and then with John Field in Moscow.

In 1810 she made her debut in Warsaw and the same year married a wealthy landowner, Josef Szymanowska. During the next five years she became very popular and was in great demand as a concert pianist. Her husband highly disapproved of her career, and her frequent appearances were offensive to him. Maria finally decided to separate from him, taking their three children with her in 1820. In 1822 she was appointed court pianist in Russia.

Many of Maria's piano compositions were published during her lifetime. Her works were admired by Liszt and Chopin. In fact, Chopin attended her concerts in Warsaw. Robert Schumann spoke highly of her in his book on musicians. Maria wrote 113 compositions, including chamber and vocal music and nearly 90 piano works, which she performed in her concerts throughout Europe.

Maria suddenly fell ill with cholera on the afternoon of July 23, 1831. She died the following morning and was buried in what is now St. Petersburg.

Nocturne

Maria Agata Szymanowska (1789–1831)

Fanny Cecile Mendelssohn Hensel ———

(1805–1847)

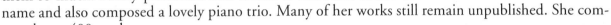

Fanny Cecile Mendelssohn Hensel was born November 14, 1805, in Hamburg, Germany. Fanny was a child prodigy who grew up in a wealthy family. Her mother began teaching her piano along with her brother Felix, who was four years younger than Fanny. By the time she was thirteen years old, Fanny could play the entire Well-tempered Clavier by J. S. Bach by memory! Her brother Felix began to perform in public at age nine and was composing when he was eleven. Although Felix was in the limelight, Fanny kept up her musical study alongside her brother. In the publication "Songs Without Words," composed by her brother, are six of Fanny's compositions: Op. 8, Nos. 2, 3, and 12, and Op. 9, Nos. 7, 10, and 12. She composed those six songs under his name because Felix liked them so much. Fanny published four books of melodies in her own name and also composed a lovely piano trio. Many of her works still remain unpublished. She composed over 400 works.

On October 3, 1829, Fanny married the Prussian court painter Wilhelm Hensel. He encouraged her composing, but it was her brother Felix who was opposed to her pieces being published. Fanny only played once in public, at a charity event, in 1838. It simply was not proper in those days for women to perform in public. Fanny was a leading participant at the family's private Sunday afternoon concert series.

Fanny and Felix were extremely close. Felix valued her judgment and musical advice and used to say that she played better than he did. She constantly promoted his work. Fanny died suddenly while rehearsing a performance of his Walpurgisnacht in the family auditorium on May 17, 1847, in Berlin, Germany. Felix fainted when he heard of her death and never regained his full energy. He died six months later. A theme of her music is engraved on the tombstone where she is buried.

Mélodie, Op. 4, No. 2

Fanny Cecile Mendelssohn Hensel (1805–1847)

Mélodie, Op. 5, No. 4

Fanny Cecile Mendelssohn Hensel (1805–1847)

Clara Wieck Schumann

(1819–1896)

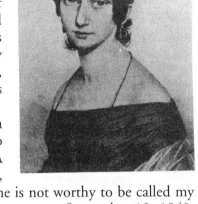

Clara Wieck Schumann was born in Leipzig on September 13, 1819. Her father was a well-known music teacher and composer who taught and pushed his talented daughter. She gave her first concert at the age of nine. By the time she was eighteen, Clara was second only to Franz Liszt among European pianists. She was the first to introduce Chopin's music to Germany; the first to play the Appassionata Sonata by Beethoven in Vienna on January 7, 1838; and the first to introduce many of Robert Schumann's works to the public.

Robert Schumann took piano lessons from Clara's father. Clara and Robert became friends, and as she grew older their friendship blossomed into love. Her father opposed the thought of marriage. A long struggle continued until she was of legal age. Mr. Wieck said, "If Clara marries Schumann, I would say upon my deathbed that she is not worthy to be called my daughter." Finally, Robert and Clara married without her father's consent on September 12, 1840, the day before her twenty-first birthday. The wedding was at ten o'clock in the morning in a little country church at Schonefeld. Just Clara's mother and their faithful friend, Ernst Becker, came with them. After they were married by the minister, the carriage drove them back to town, where a privileged group of friends were waiting to greet them.

After the successful performance of Robert's First Symphony and the arrival of their first child, Clara's father wrote them a letter of conciliatory words. During Christmas of 1843, Robert and Clara visited him for a family reunion.

Clara managed to continue her piano concerts and raise seven children. She composed many songs that she dedicated to her dear husband, Robert. Clara died on May 20, 1896, about forty years after her husband's death.

Präludium II, Op. 16

Clara Wieck Schumann (1819–1896)

Mazurka, Op. 6, No. 5

Clara Wieck Schumann (1819–1896)

Andante con sentimento

Clara Wieck Schumann (1819–1896)

Teresa Carreño

(1853–1917)

Teresa Carreño was born in Caracas, Venezuela in 1853. She studied piano with her aristocratic father, then, in 1864, they moved to New York. Her father somehow was embezzled on board the ship of his $80,000 cash fortune, so he decided to market his talented daughter in America. A child prodigy, she made her debut in New York at the age of eight. She studied with Louis Moreau Gattschalk and Mathias, both of whom studied with Chopin. When Teresa was ten years old, President Lincoln requested that she come to the White House to play for him. She played a Bach Prelude and Fugue for the president. At the age of sixteen she was summoned to play before Queen Victoria. On that occasion, Teresa wore a long gown for the first time.

Teresa was married for the first time when she was just seventeen years old to the violinist Emile Sauret. Teresa later said that she did not love him but got married only to prevent him from carrying out his threat of committing suicide if she did not marry him. After a hectic year of marriage, a daughter was born. Then, when the baby was just three days old, Teresa's husband kidnapped the baby! Sauret gave the baby to his two sisters who were living in Germany. The child legally belonged to the father, and Teresa was helpless to do anything about it. A divorce followed. She did not see her daughter for thirty-six years.

When Teresa was twenty-three, she married an opera singer who later pawned her jewels to pay his gambling debts. They had two children before they were divorced. Teresa moved to Berlin, where she began concertizing again. Her turbulent personal life was somehow made tolerable through her music. One evening she played the Concerto in A minor by Grieg, who was in the audience! He came to her after the concert, kissed her hands, and said, "Madame, my name is Grieg. I never knew I had created so beautiful a thing."

Teresa taught piano lessons and composed. One of her famous students was Edward MacDowell. She premiered his Piano Concerto in D minor in 1888. Amy Beach dedicated her piano concerto to Teresa. Her last appearance with an orchestra in the United States was with the New York Philharmonic Society on December 8, 1916. She died the following year.

Le Sommeil de l'Enfant, Op. 35

Berceuse

Teresa Carreño (1853–1917)

Intermezzo – Scherzo, Op. 34

Teresa Carreño (1853–1917)

Un Reve En Mer, Op. 28

Meditation

Teresa Carreño (1853–1917)

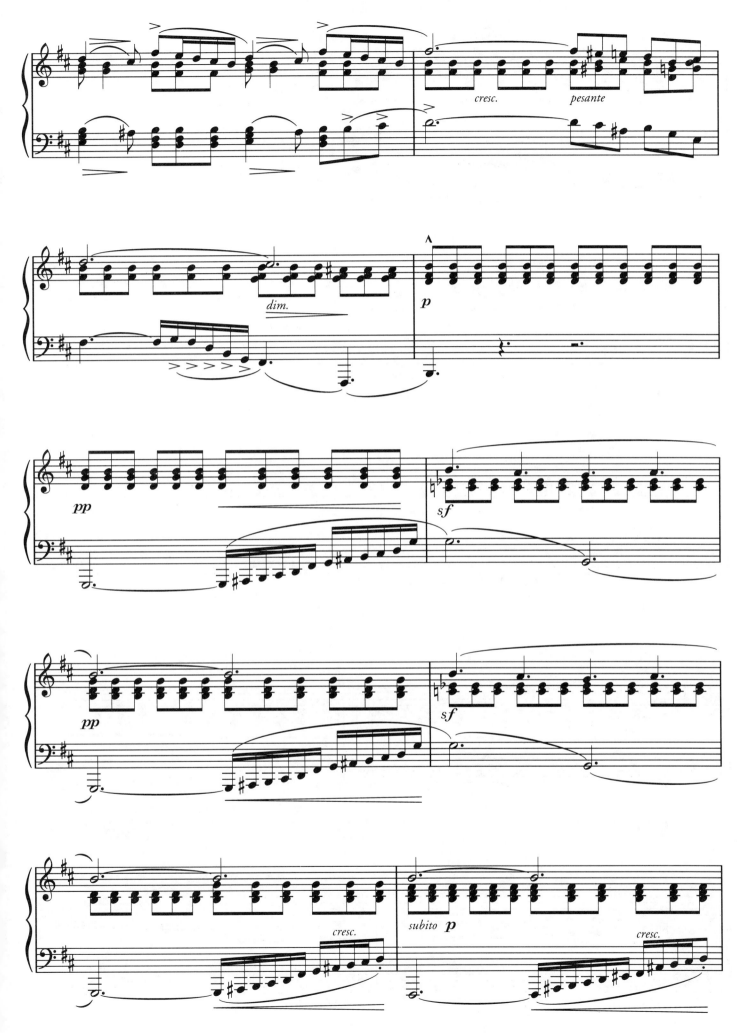

Deux Esquisses Italiennes Venise, Op. 33

Reverie—Barcarola

Teresa Carreño (1853–1917)

Cécile Chaminade

(1857–1944)

écile Chaminade was born in Paris on August 8, 1857. When she was eight years old, the famous French composer Bizet visited the Chaminade home. Cécile played one of her compositions for him, and he was amazed. Her parents took his advice and found her the best teachers in Paris. Cécile studied with Le Couppey, Savart, and Benjamin Godard. She wrote some church music as a child.

When Cécile was eighteen years old, she gave her first public concert and then began touring all over Europe, playing many of her own compositions. Her piano pieces number over two hundred, yet her most famous piece is the lovely Scarf Dance, Op. 37, No. 3, which sold millions of copies.

She made her American debut in 1908 with the Philadelphia Orchestra, performing her Concerstuck of 1896. Cécile was one of the first women to make a career of composing, and she also appeared as a conductor. She died in Monte Carlo in 1944.

Scarf Dance, Op. 37

Pas Des Echarpes

3rd Air De Ballet

Cécile Chaminade (1857–1944)

Mouviment modéré de Valse 𝅗𝅥. = 54

Pierrette, Op. 41

Air de Ballet

Cécile Chaminade (1857–1944)

Minuetto, Op. 23

Cécile Chaminade (1857–1944)

La Morena, Op. 67

Cécile Chaminade (1857–1944)

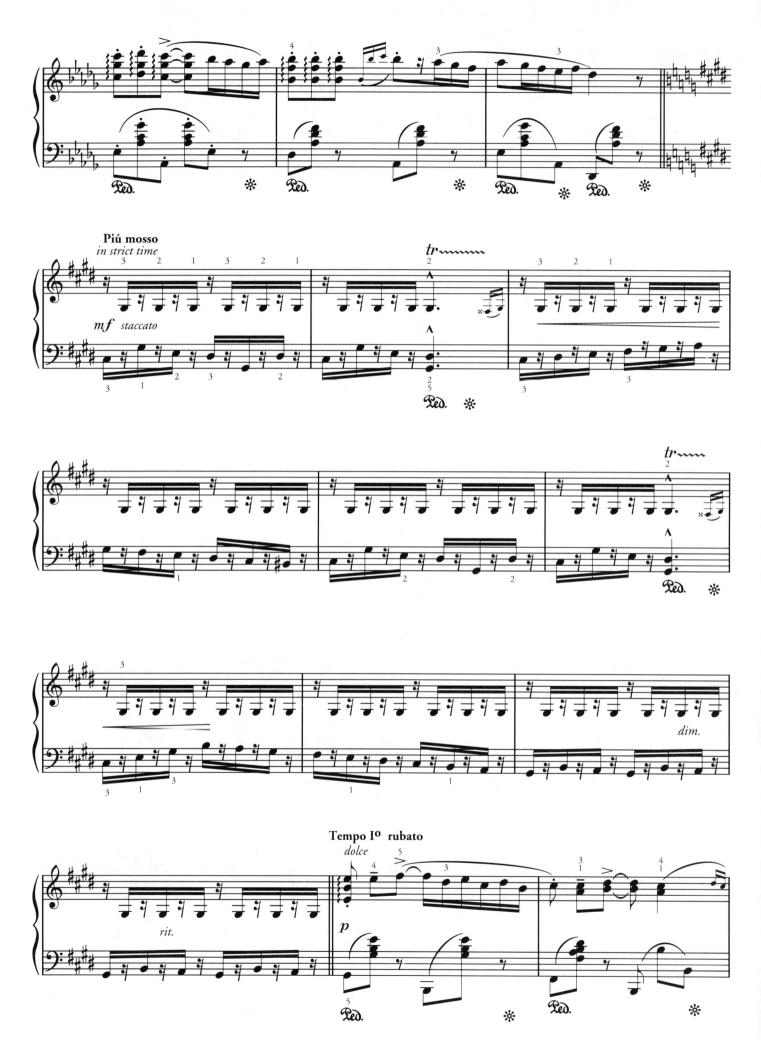

Lili Boulanger ———————

(1893–1918)

Lili Boulanger was born in Paris on August 21, 1893. Her father was Ernest Boulanger, a famous composer and professor of singing at the Conservatoire National de Musique in Paris. He had won the Grand Prix de Rome in 1835. He married a nineteen-year-old Russian princess when he was sixty-two years old and was seventy-nine when Lili was born. Lili was born into a very musical family. Her grandmother was a popular singer at the Opera-Comique, and her grandfather had been a cellist with the King's Chapel. Lili's older sister, Nadia, taught her piano. Lili also learned to play a number of other instruments, among them violin, organ, and harp.

Lili became the first woman to win the Grand Prix de Rome in music. The year was 1913 (seventy-eight years after her father had won it), and Lili was just twenty years old when her cantata "Faust et Helene" won. Camille Saint-Säens was on the jury of the Prix de Rome. Lili was a brilliant composer. During her short life she composed many lovely pieces. She died of tuberculosis at the age of twenty-five on March 15, 1918, in Mezy, France.

D'un vieux Jardin

à Lily Jumel

Lili Boulanger (1893–1918)

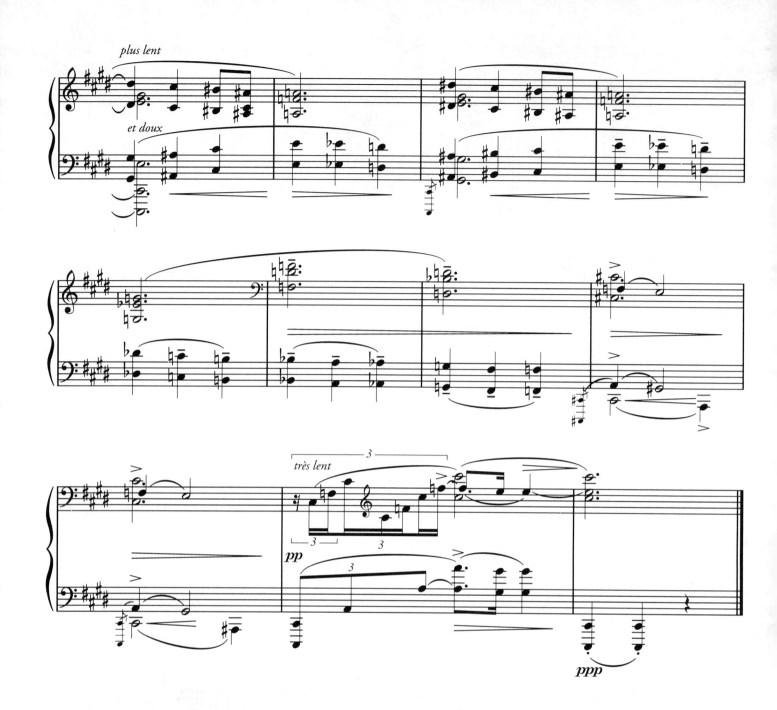

Amy Marcy Beach

(1867–1944)

Amy Marcy Beach was born in Henniker, New Hampshire, on September 5, 1867. Her mother was her first piano teacher. Amy was a child prodigy who composed her first song at the age of four. She was very sound sensitive and heard music in colors. To Amy, the key of E-flat was pink, and the key of A-flat was blue. She accurately notated the bird songs for a famous scientist when she was just ten years old. Amy remained interested in bird songs all her life and composed "The Hermit Thrush at Morn" after hearing a hermit thrush sing outside her window at the MacDowell Colony one summer.

Amy made her debut at the age of sixteen with the Boston Symphony Orchestra. When she was eighteen she married Dr. H.H.A. Beach, a wealthy doctor who was older than her father. They had a happy twenty-five-year marriage, during which time Amy composed most of her major orchestral works.

Amy composed the piano Concerto in C-sharp minor, the Gaelic Symphony, numerous vocal solos, choral anthems, chamber works, cantatas, and hundreds of piano solos. Amy performed her concertos all over the world and concertized throughout the United States.

She died in New York City on December 27, 1944. Her great music lives on and inspires us. The following is a quote from *Mrs. H.H.A. Beach: The First Woman Composer of America:* "The monuments of a nation mark the progress of its civilization, but its intelligence and education are qualified by its music."

A Hermit Thrush at Morn, Op. 92, No. 2

"I heard from morn to morn a merry thrush
Sing hymns of rapture, while I drank the sound
With joy."

J. Clare

Amy Marcy Beach (1867–1944)

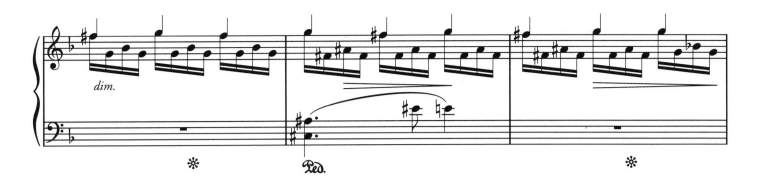

126   Amy Marcy Beach

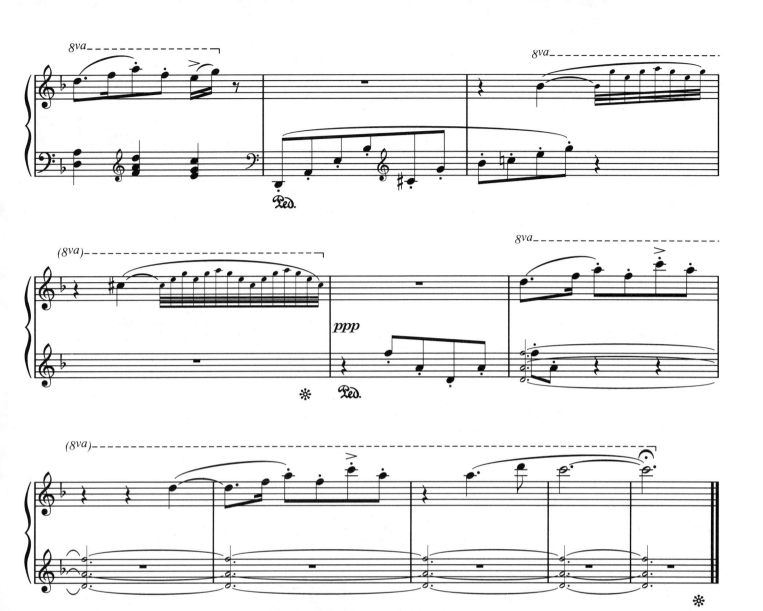

Exiles, Op. 64, No. 3

Amy Marcy Beach (1867–1944)

With Dog-teams, Op. 64, No. 4

Amy Marcy Beach (1867–1944)

sempre staccato

Ped. ✻ Ped. ✻

Ped. ✻

Ped. ✻ Ped. ✻ Ped. ✻

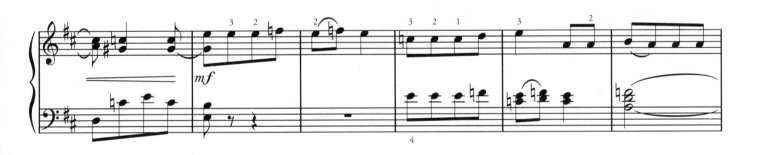

The Old Chapel by Moonlight, Op. 106

Amy Marcy Beach (1867–1944)

Gail Smith

(b. 1943)

Author Gail Smith was born in Bridgeport, Connecticut, on January 26, 1943. Both of her grandparents were born in Sweden. Gail's father, Carl Erick Johnson, sang tenor in the church choir. Her mother, Ethel, played the piano and had Gail start piano lessons.

Gail Smith received her Bachelor of Fine Arts degree from Florida Atlantic University. She has taught piano students from the age of 3 to 96! Her blind student, Ivan, was seen on national TV.

Giving musical lecture recitals by portraying the composer's wife has been an effective way to reach audiences with the history of music. Gail has portrayed Marian MacDowell and Anna Magdalena Bach. She gives many workshops and concerts throughout the States as well as in Germany and Japan.

Gail has two daughters and is married to C. Alonza Smith. They live in Fort Lauderdale, Florida. Her life has revolved around her family, church and music. Gail was the pianist of the famed Coral Ridge Presbyterian church for many years. She has been active in many organizations including being National music chairman of the NLAPW and President of the local branch. She is a member of The Freedoms Foundation of Valley Forge, National Music Teachers Association, and Federation of Music Clubs.

Gail's works include many piano solos, choral works, a piano trio, a composition for four pianos and numerous vocal solos. She has arranged hundreds of hymns, Indian melodies, and folk tunes from many countries. Gail has composed twelve piano palindromes, which are her trademark. These unique solos can be played backwards as well as forwards and sound the same.

Improvisation

Gail Smith (1943–   )